The Bridge at Uji

Also by Tom Lowenstein:

Poetry

Filibustering in Samsara. The Many Press, 1987
Ancestors and Species. Shearsman Books, 2005
Conversation with Murasaki. Shearsman Books, 2009
From Culbone Wood – in Xanadu. Shearsman Books, 2013

On Tikiġaq History

The Things That Were Said of Them. University of California Press, 1992
Ancient Land: Sacred Whale. Bloomsbury; Farrar Strauss and Giroux, 1993
Ultimate Americans. University of Alaska Press, 2008
Tikiġaq, an Early History. North Slope Borough, 2018
The Structure of Days Out. Shearsman Books, 2020

Tom Lowenstein

The Bridge at Uji

Shearsman Books

First published in the United Kingdom in 2022 by
Shearsman Books
P O Box 4239
Swindon
SN3 9FN

Shearsman Books Ltd Registered Office
30–31 St. James Place, Mangotsfield, Bristol BS16 9JB
(this address not for correspondence)

www.shearsman.com

ISBN 978-1-84861-797-1

Copyright © Tom Lowenstein, 2022.
The right of Tom Lowenstein to be identified as the author of this work has been asserted by him in accordance with the Copyrights, Designs and Patents Act of 1988.
All rights reserved.

ACKNOWLEDGEMENTS

With sincerest thanks to these people especially
who gave me encouragement:

Anna Lowenstein, Lonka,
Bob Saxton, Richard Bready, Ewan Smith.

The cover image is taken from a photograph of *The River Bridge at Uji*, a Japanese six-fold screen from the Momoyama Period in the collection of the Nelson-Atkins Museum of Art, Kansas City.

The Bridge at Uji

Preface

Uji is now a suburb to the south of Kyoto and its bridge over the river was first constructed in the 10th century. At one end sits a modern representation of Murasaki who introduced the bridge into the last chapters of her novel, translated by Arthur Waley as *The Tale of Genji*.

I sat by the bridge for half a day some years back watching the water flow in one direction while foot passengers and traffic moved across at right angles.

On return to London, the physicality of the bridge returned qua metaphor, both as expressed by that particular bridge passage and as suggested by all modes of transition – though these might shift. In the poems that follow that metaphorical gesture repeats and may be interpreted idiosyncratically by separate readers.

1.

Of all the directions in which
the bridge could lead us
there is just one which has been built in,
offering the illusion of simplicity.
So gratefully, we'll take this.

2.

On the far side of the bridge
lodges the caretaker and guide.
But you must surrender to the unknown
before arriving at your question.

3.

Yes, I shouted in the direction
of her cubicle and have glimpsed
fugitive proposals for a reply.
It was then I understood that she too
was uncertain of my purpose
and was herself hanging on in confusion.

4.

Some people I know cross lightheartedly and disdain to make a fuss. There are others for whom a direct line to the other side represents the ultimate labyrinth.

5.

In which connection there can only be a shameful solitude. Nobody is going to empathise with a trajectory which appears so fatuously simple but which opens an almighty gulf.

6.

There are certain damselflies whose
wing pattern you absorb only once
they have emerged from the shadow
of the arches where they'd sheltered.

They are weak but valiant creatures.
And I identify with them thus
without their acknowledgement.

7.

I am haunted by the Pali term
pabbajati, 'he/she goes forth'.
I.e from domestic security
to fill space
with the constituent of the body and coming
to the bridge like any
phenomenon of the constructed world
which must be encountered
for what surely it must be
in some kind of reality.

8.

Shakespeare, given that it is a
projection of the imagination,
has traversed the bridge.
Metaphorically at least.
This is where fools all caper with their songs.
And dispense crazy
wisdom to the earnest.

9.

It's deep, this Nothing.
But it doesn't take much
to convince me that on
the whole it's a waste of time.

10.

The man lying in his urine
the young Buddha saw was
a concoction of the deities
he didn't anyway believe in.
And there are people, these days,
who still lie in urine or that of others.
Humanity has invented hygiene
for the privileged few – and where is the virtue in searching
       further?

11.

For those already half-way across
and who halt their steps in panic,
it is a benign disillusion and most
great art you have studied
on the near side represents
a serene contemplation of
that inevitable oscillation.

12.

'The floating bridge of dreams'
is what Murasaki called it.
                              Perhaps
on the one hand the bridge is part
of the river. On the other, among several,
to speak of this and that side represents
a comfortable illusion.
                              Never fear.
We must make the attempt anyway.
Or perhaps she was writing
about an underside reflection
that amalgamated one illusion with another.

13.

There is another reality whose claims
are significant and their persistence daunting.
And what difference, anyway, whether or not
I transcribe these lucubrations?

14.

Every step I take on the bridge
and even as I attempt escaping it
proclaims the assumption
that personally I matter. All life forms
require space in which to express
themselves without exclusion
or obliteration of the other.
Thus the way forward remains
conditioned by ambiguity.

15.

A bronze statue of Murasaki
stands at the near edge of the bridge.
She's incapable of moving.
This is probably the easiest way
to get across. But she has
no desire to do so.

16.

A counter-colleague confirms
that he has initiated
an underground project:
and this is to use the dimension
of the river ipse to undercut
the world of light and air.

17.

The tedium of crossing.
And footfall of a million ghosts
that echo
on the darker rushing.
Nothing lasts. It is merely interrupted.
One thing after another.

18.

Non-existence on the other side
that it is inaccurate
to describe as peaceful,

for the need to travel
and superstitions about it
have amalgamated on this side only,

and the authorities have forgotten
to pave the starting point
which has become trampled and muddy.

19.

Finding the beautiful in simplicity. Thus language is made redundant and we crave silence to comprehend this.

20.

Perpetual motion
for a relatively short period
is a fate we share.

To get stuck is a misfortune. But
even that may be part of the continuity.

21.

All life demands is that
we should act with courtesy and
companionship with what grows.

The beautiful unnoticed power of seeds.
And the seeds' perseverance.

22.

The white stripe on the hawk's side
differentiating
its peculiar species though
it may not know this.

23.

Plunged into the creative
maelstrom of conditionality.

Space is enormous.
We are left still with silence from
which conditions are arising.

24.

A petal falls. A grandmother,
in synchrony, expires.
We mourn dutifully and with
briefly expressed sentiment.

Death, come closer. We need
your pain to go on living.

25.

Gratefully, clumsily, I embrace
the emptiness I come from
and to which like
everyone I shall return.

A companionship of nescience,
neither pleasant nor otherwise.

26.

Gratifying to observe so many kinds of bee visit the primroses that have seeded themselves in cracks between the stones we laid between the gooseberry bushes and the tool shed we converted to a summer house. They are fastidiously busy and understand enough about nourishment and colour to sustain themselves so long as we refrain from interrupting them.

27.

The funny looking geezer reflected
in this hospital mirror, a few white
whiskers imperfectly shaven from an
earlier attempt before the taxi's arrival.

Is he really the same person
as the four-year-old snapped
smiling with his father and sister
when news from Europe had just broken?

As if we could anticipate our years anew
and contemplate the future.

28.

Now in recovery from a remote seeming
head injury, I am in a condition to weep.

And while the world does not require my pity,
the lacrimae rerum of universal
existence is more contingent
than when my head was filled
with what I imagined to be significant.

29.

Lacrimae rerum. The tears
of things. Or tears inherent.

But there is no psychologist
to explain to us whether
the weeping is intrinsic
but withheld, or if the same
phenomena provoke in us
a lachrymose reaction
and that this represents
a psychological projection.

30.

Sparrows that muck round in what
look like dead branches but which
I pray could be impregnated by proleptic
egg laying albeit somewhere else presumably.

31.

Thrashing, or perhaps threshing
in the stream. There's not
much left for any individual once
they have consumed their part of it.

The stream proceeds.
It goes nowhere. It is static.
Hard to coincide with paradox
of movement and of nothing.

32.

I might continue writing
if the words hadn't reached
the furthest and most extreme
boundary already.

Oh how they scuttled once
from the left.
How is it now they've piled
sulking
in the left hand margin?

33.

The more unstable
underfoot and the abyss
profound as are the
upper fathoms and as empty,

the more cheerfully
I try calling to the other side.
And whether or not a response
is forthcoming, it will
be my echo from which
I must derive reassurance.

34.

I will not claim there to be
an inherent weirdness,
but these kookie vibes
are impossible in
ordinary language
to interpret,

and I must connive
with the comedy of
symbolism albeit that the laughs
no doubt represent an evasion
that will take us to our graves in
shared cerements of the unspoken.

35.

Their lives peter out.
They are forgotten, their mistakes,
minor successes and deceptions
no more or less significant than
our own small divagations
between this and that presumption.

The silent clatter of masks
I leave behind me in a ripple.
In a sibilation.
This too has limits.
Vertebrae with the inertia of water.

Oh, the vulnerable and scarcely
half born persona to which I too
am a stranger.

That which remains unseen
may be said not
in the first place to have existed.

36.

Desire. Desiderate. Consider.
Etymologically re-traceable
in Virgil to the sidera.
'When I consider how my light is spent.'
When I adjust my wants
that with such insignificance
inform my ego,
then I too note that vast
enduring down gaze and unseeing presence.

37.

A mixed blessing
this member of male equipment,
albeit the ambiguity of
its presence was to become
a relatively late
feature of consciousness.

Earlier in my confusion,
I read cautionary Yoruba fables
about the Trickster deity
Eshu Elegba and of deceptively
amenable river bridges that
he erected from his person
only to crack them
in mid-passage as travellers
of both sexes
ventured a short cut
across the Sokoto.

Possession of this physiological apparatus,
once a fountain of occasional
and intermittent happiness,
becomes in later experience
something of an inconvenience,
if not a hazard.

There are PhDs to be acquired by advanced and helpful,
frequently well-recompensed, high status practitioners.

This doesn't, however, render them immune to the conditions they explore, whether or not progressively. Unless they happen to be women. Although this is unlikely.

38.

In despite the bridge trajectory
which leapfrogged
the implacable architecture
of water, I achieved nonetheless
a moment of balance and privacy

and no longer was alone
in mythological central Japan
but had been admitted to
this almost invisible divagation:
It was April
on a grass bank
in the foothills of the French alps
where a patch
of blue hepatica had marked
a temporary presence.

On return to Uji
the onrush of the bridge continued.
The water was as ever.
Everything's in motion.
And the bridge was no exception.

39.

The viola part.
Given Haydn and Mozart
agreed these lines were worth writing out,
then you can take pride in your contribution.

It remains inconspicuous and modest,
with minor and occasionally
daring interventions
somewhere between the
violin G string and the higher cello registers.

How comfortable this reticence, this quiet residence.
But it is an illusory reassurance
that companion players
won't have noticed your contribution
as you'd hoped they might have.

40.

How to resolve
the insoluble conundrum
which is known but
unnamed, a threat of
strangulation, no hand
on the throat, but tight
contusion of the glottal.

41.

The is-ness of the geese,
the swans and even
of the parakeets we disapprove of.

Neither is the twittering of sparrows
and their probably meaningful
inter-communication lost on me,
as each syllable disappears into the racket.

42.

The incomprehensible
that makes me weep so.
Multiplicity and oblivion.
The old man forgets everything.
So muchness to be burdened tackling
and little comprehended.
A black hole, each of us,
sucking in as much of the entirety
for which in the body
there is space available.
But then we will for ever be out of date,
and the grand children will have their unknowable posterity.

43.

i.
Oh, begins my little poem,
suggesting an expostulation
of a self-regard, of individuality.

But the path that cuts through the burial ground
and divides it, as did the myth God.
Everything that so mysteriously evolved
in Genesis, reveals a brave defiance
of a long winter gestation
under broad crisp plane leaves
and the eroded inscriptions
that fall round still optimistically
on lop-sided grave stones
on which lichen thrives
where the stone mason chiseled at an angle.

ii.
Neither the snowdrops that come first
nor the little daffs
that have survived a hob-nailed quatrain
have much in common with the melancholy
that's balanced with the courage of reaching upward.

Green and white. Then sourly lemon.
A wind that sneaps them
vainly makes its passage.

44.

Convincingly, as Sterne
has shown, there's no straight line
from an intention.
Every act entails a variation.[1]

---

[1] Could Uncle Toby have made it across without the whirligig of Trim's walking stick which indelibly has been inscribed on the atlas of progress: a globe off axis?

45.

And as Heine opined:
our thoughts are random,
whatever care
post hoc we take to pattern them.

46.

No-one, luckily, has noticed my tendency to sub-vocalise
and how I might be heard to breathe across the uvula 'Fuck off'.

My interlocutor remains an earlier self: one whose solecisms
require the sort of reprimand demanded by seniority.
Nice old gentlemen refrain from out-loud language blips.

47.

Anything I may have learned I have forgotten.
What I believed was a shadow of someone else's figment.
Thought derived from brain structure and interaction with
    phenomena.
Now what I know is that I do not know, and even this is relative.

48.

Serene contemplation of the possible.
The negative drops away.
Its fall to the pole opposite
engenders a condition of Nothing
from we shall start again.

49.

The sky is complex
and not just on account of our projections.
Still, the strata reveal themselves
in transitory archaeological series.
Because nothing is there, we avoid digging.
This would take us too high.
And it would resemble astrology.

50.

Round this fogscape of Monet
the wall from which it emerges has dissipated.
And we resign ourselves
to an existence of impressions.

51.

The air and the water
are composed of the same green immateriality.
Still, everything is made of interchangeable components.
Because I live in doubt
I allow myself a parallel counterfeit.
Diffusion followed by dissolution.

52.

The Houses of Parliament are revealed
by Monet not as solid.
But as mutable in half light.
Thus a democracy of phenomena
escaping continually from itself.

53.

Form, as early Buddhists determined,
exists in a whirligig of coexistent phenomena.
But to choose one as an object of study
one pursues a preliminary divagation
into interpenetrative media.

Such mysteries are inversive.
Expressing the flavours
of childhood and old age
in the identical reflective teaspoon.

54.

Le soleil dans le brouillard.
Thus Monet's note to his dealer.
Meanwhile, the sun has dissipated
the fog vista and gone down irregularly.

55.

Enough of these paradoxes.
And engage with the simplicity
of seeing double
without elements
of surprise or pretension.

But don't be bitter.
Most things go wrong for most people.

56.

Is that thing an actual Monet?
No, it's the lift door
which has been the object
of a kicking.

57.

'Everything is the same,'
you said.
Good cooking perhaps exempted.

58.

Oh long, beautiful sentence,
with your complexity of parentheses.
I have travelled with you
without divagating
from your mesmeric ordination.

59.

So have I failed
in all things I can think of,
imagining there to be an angel
taking notes on the periphery
with a dislocated feather.

60.

Seneca, however, with his
indifference to posterity
has been remembered.

61.

The seed of a fishing boat
lying low in the water.
It might be a ripple.

62.

That this was madness
was confirmed by the primrose stem.
Its innocuous flowering.

63.

But to no-one,
only to this tray of weeds,
have I expressed
degeneration.

64.

Void surfing.
Excavation of the ultimate
with a persona.

65.

If there are ultimate powers
out there or even within reach,
that struggle with each other,
and which genius experiences
on the body: those are invisible
to the smaller people to whom I belong
and who are my comarades.

66.

For like the cat, I am happy
with a few smallish things
in my porridge helping.

67.

What is man? asked the psalmist.
Neither can the rest of us make it out.
'Nor women neither,' as false friends aside-ed.

The whale sweeping krill, still,
into the dimension of its hunger,
surges northward.

Neither is there a god
who has questioned the evolution of matter.
Crustacea printed on flint
from deep time under foot still.

68.

Oh you beautiful sentences
in a long, impressive narrative.
You have left the reader smiling.

69.

You will perhaps explain to me.
I know nothing.

70.

Come now. Entrance us with
the Mozartian in your tragedy.
Sadness, unlike Mozart's, superficial .

71.

Don't hammer quite so
on the keyboard.
You will wake the half-dead souls
who take comfort in their limbo.

72.

From the woodpecker's
perspective, it's a good enough environment,
the mortality of this ash tree.

73.

If anything touches me,
that which stays remote
may go on touching.

This quartet with piano
thunders past, complete
in self-enclosure.
A phenomenon beyond awareness
that's known itself
since long composition.

74.

Bless you, my door.
You have opened with such generosity.
Whether there's anything
inside, I may learn from the threshold.

75.

It's despairing (dust hath beauty)
comfort-giving gaiety,
the sort elaborated by Ecclesiastes' priesthood.

76.

Oh, I'm like everyone else more or less.
This and that work OK.
But mostly it's undeveloped.

77.

Milk rising in a cloud
from tea-cup bottom.
It knows to mix without a hostess.
The inconspicuous are happiest.

78.

The viola idiom again.
You'll be better pleased
without an encore.

79.

Lives improvised and then forgotten.
Ours no different.
We scratch a few marks
and time erodes them.
The erosion of itself eroded.

80.

Those suffering today:
Yemeni children,
abused Burmese Muslims,
Assam monsoon victims.
Your feather-bedded melancholy
and its Western pedigree
is harder to interpret.

81.

That I've been traipsing
in search of an Ur-text:
that I can't deny nor justify.
The language of that text no longer exists.
And perhaps anyway it was almost as transient
as the phone texts I have learned to make
and which today's practitioners
have rendered obsolete already.

82.

The island of the self.
But developed without purpose,
unconscious of its development,
of the surrounding archipelago
and without a map.

This is not treasure island
and there's no sweet pit to dig,
or climax to return from.

I'd like, having consulted both a renaissance atlas
and a more recently engineered one, to re-start.

But natural law obstructs such rethinks.
And so I accept we spin on, wandering.

83.

Wanting to drink glaze.

Such skinny bits of seaweed
and these thin-etched carrot slices.

How swiftly
otherwise the glaze might slip down
in the drinking.

84.

If the meaning is hidden,
then let it remain so.
We have dined on the explicit
and are still to digest it.

85.

B minor and then G minor.
I have played them without understanding.
And if they have import,
it's this escapes my bow.

86.

'All thanks, O God, for not
making me like those other people.
And more thanks, even,
for not making them like me.'

87.

A Muse sometimes will herself play
an accompanying guitar-like instrument.
I have noted this on a vase.
But have not myself visited Helicon.

88.

Nor did I understand
quite how frightening it might have been
to have come face to face
with one of the Gorgon sisters,
without the mirror on me
I'd been accustomed to carry.

89.

I saw this woman in the museum café
doing all she could to cheer up
and to manage her depressive husband.
That was quite a lesson in keeping herself going.

90.

'Would you like this one?'
'No, I'd prefer that one.'
'But I've already offered you that.'
This dialogue in Switzer Deutsch,
though the interaction was universal.

91.

I could show you some Greek vases,
but you are forbidden to handle them.
The gods and heroes run past empty handed.
You can hear their foreskins whistle.

92.

This was just one genre.
The variety within it,
however, expressed everything.

93.

Towards life's end, finally
apostrophising flowers,
the fragility of whose ancestors
you addressed as your contemporary,
so temporary,
although you didn't know that.

94.

This boy's relationship with toys
may always have been ambivalent.
Then his connection with them
as well as with objects of disdain
became coercive. Oh, the punishment
of a brayed trumpet!

95.

Arriving at life's end.
Not a status to be regretted.
But the hole where you were reflected
not by your own witness,
not reflecting.

96.

This is what freezes doubt.
The enigma of having to go forward.
Entropy threatens.
Still there's an element that persists,
as though it were energy itself mattered.
So I have refused to give up,
and I give thanks both to forebears, to contemporaries
and to younger people who know better than me,
that I don't live in a desert.
There is no shame in this persuasion.
It's all right to go on singing.

97.

How weak and mouldy
these lines will appear.
Not even assembled
in a well-funded archive
by well-meaning and underpaid library assistants.

98.

On the viola d'amore,
thus you have set my heart strings'
secondary layer (in sympathy) vibrating.

99.

What I disdain is my very dislike.
How to transcend that involves
abandoning the disdain reaction
and then to view this also with indifference.

100.

They understand, these days,
scientific people,
more than the old poets dreamed of.
Still there are those of us
with our heads in the past
who comprehend neither.

101.

Oh, I belong in that tradition.
Its very existence being
an exclusive context,
the lovelier for my relegation
to the margin.

102.

Long after I'd abandoned the prospect of a crossing,
still underfoot. The texture of the knots, grain and splinters
created the impact of their fantasy.
But the notion of a passage, for all its inaccessibility,
remained what I imagined to be the desideratum.

103.

Not striving to save the world
in gusts of ambition:
merely a struggle to inscribe sentences.

104.

Oh, the trouble I can project
into this otherwise clarifying lacuna.

105.

Do I love this mountain
for an eminence
that's excluded me?

106.

Where you are
destined to suffer nightmares.
But then on waking
with the reward of a clear view.

107.

Not till I have scribbled
ten inconsequential verses
can I revert
to a relaxation position,
which is the nearest I can get
both to the afterlife
and a desirable instead-of.
What the cats accomplish:
which is a disquisition of indifference.

108.

These moments of ambiguous
contemplation. Is it these
you would revisit, or indeed make
the assumption of a more generalized interest?
I don't think so. Doubt, surely,
being a component.
And the abiding negativity.

109.

Fear, after all, of having taken
a forthright position,
is nothing, in your view,
altogether positive
and without its tincture of regret
and the ascription of others
of a decisive experience.
But you know yourself also
to be a divided being,
that 'poor forked' entity
whose shape remains emblematic.

110.

Ah, the still posture of these larger birds
and the frantic pecking of the sparrows I feed,
twitching as these do with the conflicting energies
of being happy in the moment and getting safely away with it.

111.

So pleasant it is for a moment
to sit in the sun,
while to acknowledge its transcience
without altogether repining.

112.

And while I sensed this [was local] (MS illegible)
I'd entered universal time
and our distance from the planet Sol
represented global equidistance.

113.

Ode to Silence

A café in Madrid.
Or was it Weimar?

Still I'm with you, gracious lady.
And I'm also perhaps She,
in company and absence, both.

114.

I heard these ducks yapping.
And I guessed their meaning.
But I would have to yap as long as they do
to render myself intelligible.

115.

Oh the iniquity, in the context
of global desperation,
to be scribbling these verses.

Perhaps not adding to the culture.
But contributing, at least,
to an alignment with its potential.

116.

The holy icons we've been taught to imagine,
and the idealized shapes
that contrast with such sculptural exactness
to our absence of defined form:
I would model at least my appearance
on this sensitively realized stonework
in the paint of Mantegna and Bellini,
whatever the turmoil
that underlies the precision of that stillness.

117.

The bee in its hurry
jogs the celandine and pulmonaria.
It's the same with sparrows just outside my window:
they speed round, twitching, and then:
'Sorry, I've a million things to do still…'
No time to confer, and not a second's idleness.

www.ingramcontent.com/pod-product-compliance
Lightning Source LLC
Chambersburg PA
CBHW031634160426
43196CB00006B/413